# Indication of the Way
# into the Kingdom of Heaven

T0206873

# Indication of the Way into the Kingdom of Heaven

## An Introduction to Christian Life

Saint Innocent of Alaska

Holy Trinity Publications
The Printshop of St Job of Pochaev
Holy Trinity Monastery
Jordanville, New York

Printed with the blessing of His Eminence,
Metropolitan Hilarion, First Hierarch
of the Russian Orthodox Church Outside of Russia

Indication of the Way into Heaven
© 1952, 2013 Holy Trinity Monastery, Second edition 2013

HOLY TRINITY PUBLICATIONS
The Printshop of St Job of Pochaev
Holy Trinity Monastery
Jordanville, New York 13361-0036
www.holytrinitypublications.com

Cover photo: The Road North, Labrador
© 1987 Christopher Burkett;
West Wind Arts Inc., P.O. Box 22108,
Milwaukie, OR 97269
http://www.christopherburkett.com

ISBN: 978-0-88465-303-5 (paper)
ISBN: 978-0-88465-003-4 (ePub)
ISBN: 978-0-88465-305-9 (Mobipocket)

Library of Congress Control Number 2012950645

# CONTENTS

Saint Innocent
Metropolitan of Moscow, 1867–1879

# INTRODUCTION

People were not created merely to live here on earth like animals that disappear after their death, but to live with God and in God, and to live not for a hundred or a thousand years, but to live eternally. But only Christians can live with God: that is to say, those who rightly believe in Jesus Christ.

Everyone, whoever he may be, desires and seeks prosperity and happiness. To desire what is good for oneself and to seek prosperity or happiness is part of man's nature, and, therefore, it is not a sin or vice. But we need to know that here on earth there has not been, is not, and never will be true and perfect happiness and prosperity; for all our prosperity and happiness is only in God. No one will ever find true happiness and perfect prosperity without God or outside God.

Nothing in this world but God can fill our heart or fully satisfy our desires. A fire cannot be put out with brushwood and oil because only water will put it out. In exactly the same way, the desires of the human heart cannot be satisfied with the goods of this world because only the grace of God can quench the thirst of our desires.

Everything we desire pleases us only so long as we do not possess it; and when we get it, we soon get tired of it. Or only what we do not as yet have seems to us good and attractive; whereas all that we have, even though it is the very best, is either not enough for us or does not attract us. A good example of this is King Solomon, who, as is well known, was so rich that all the household plate and furniture in his palaces was of pure gold; he was so wise that kings came to visit him; and he was so glorious that his foes were terrified of him. Being wiser and mightier than all his contemporaries, he was able to satisfy all his wishes and desires, so that there was hardly a thing in the world that he did not possess or could not obtain. But with all this he could not satisfy his heart, and the desires of his heart wearied and tormented him far more than an ordinary man; and in the end, having tried everything in the world, he said in his writings, "Everything in this world is vanity, and nothing can satisfy our desires."

Truly, not a single earthly pleasure can satisfy our heart. We are strangers on earth, pilgrims and travelers; our home and fatherland are there in heaven, in the heavenly kingdom; and there do not exist on earth things that could perfectly satisfy our desires. Let a man own the whole world and all that is in the world, yet all that will not interest him for more than a minute, so to speak, and it will never satisfy his heart; for the heart of man can be fully satisfied only by the love of God, and therefore God alone can fill the heart and soul of man and quench the thirst of his desires.

And so, do you wish to live with God there, in the kingdom of heaven? Be an Orthodox Christian. Do you want prosperity and happiness? Seek it in God. Do you want your heart to be fully satisfied? Turn it to God from Whom you have been separated by your sins.

However, no one by himself, without Jesus Christ, can turn and draw near to God, because our sins, like a high wall, do not let us come to Him. And unless Jesus Christ in His mercy to us had come down to earth, and unless He had taken to Himself our human flesh and by His death destroyed the wall that separated us from God, everyone would have perished and not a single soul could have drawn near to God or lived with Him. For everyone is a sinner and is born in sin from his mother's womb; and even in an infant, although it knows nothing of the world and does nothing, there is already the seed of sin.

Therefore Jesus Christ is our Redeemer, Savior, Deliverer, and Benefactor. Now everyone who wants to do so can return to God and enter the kingdom of heaven.

But there is only one way into the kingdom of heaven, and that is the very way that Jesus Christ went when He lived on earth. There is no other way, and never was, and never will be, for Jesus Christ said, "I am the way"

(John 14:6). "If anyone desires to come after Me, let him deny himself, and take up his cross, and follow Me" (Matt 16:24).

And so, for every Christian, and even for every human being, it is extremely necessary to know how to find the way and how to follow it. And here I want to talk to you about this way; and although I know myself that I cannot show it to you as I ought, yet I shall try according to my powers, trusting in Jesus Christ Who can use dirt itself for healing and curing.

Now, whoever comes across my book and wants to read it will find in it nothing but a poor and feeble explanation of the way into the kingdom of heaven. But if anyone reads it through with prayer to Jesus Christ, He, being almighty, even by these words of mine can enlighten and warm the heart of the reader.

I divide my book into four parts: (1) on the benefits that Jesus Christ has granted us by His death; (2) how Jesus Christ lived on earth, and what He suffered for us; (3) the way by which we must go into the kingdom of heaven; and (4) how Jesus Christ helps us to go by this way, and how we can receive this help.

O Lord Jesus Christ, to Thee I cry: Hearken unto me, Thine unworthy servant! Enlighten my mind; grant that I may truly and clearly describe Thy way into the kingdom of glory that Thou, in Thy mercy, has granted us! Grant that those who read and listen to my words may be filled with Thy love, enlightened by Thy knowledge, and made strong by Thy power. Warm our hearts with Thy Spirit, and we shall joyfully and fervently go the way that Thou has shown us.

## POINTS OF REFLECTION

1. What does it mean to "rightly believe in Jesus Christ"?

2. Do we believe, with St Innocent, that "no one will ever find true happiness and perfect prosperity without God or outside God"? How might this belief be reflected in our daily activities?

3. "The desires of the human heart cannot be satisfied with the goods of this world." Think of examples of *the goods of this world* with which we attempt to fill our need for God.

4. How does our sin create a wall that prevents us from knowing God?

5. How do we read this, or any other Christian spiritual text, prayerfully?

# CHAPTER I

# The Blessings That Jesus Christ Has Granted Us by His Death

Before speaking of this, let us look at the blessings that Adam had in paradise before he committed sin, and at the evil that Adam suffered after he had committed sin, and with him all men.

The first man, being created in the image and likeness of God, until he had blurred the likeness of God by his self-will, was blessed in that very image and likeness of God. Just as God has no end and is eternal, so, too, was Adam created immortal. God is all-righteous, and Adam was created sinless and righteous. God is all-happy, and Adam was created happy, and his happiness could have increased day by day throughout all eternity.

Adam lived in a most beautiful paradise, in a garden planted by God Himself, where he was content with everything. He was always healthy and well, and he would never have known any kind of sickness. He was not afraid of anyone or anything. All the animals and birds obeyed him as their king. He felt neither cold nor heat. And although he labored and worked in paradise, yet he worked with pleasure and delight and did not find toil burdensome or work tiring.

His heart and soul were full of knowledge and love of God. He was always quiet and happy, and he never knew and never saw anything unpleasant, upsetting, painful, or sad. All his desires were pure, right, and in order. His memory, intellect, and all the other faculties of his soul were perfect. And being innocent and pure, he always lived with God and conversed with Him, and God loved him as His favorite son. In short, Adam was in paradise, and paradise was in Adam.

Now, if Adam had not broken the commandment of his Creator, he would have been happy himself, and all his descendants would have always been happy, too. But Adam sinned before God and broke His law, and the easiest law; and for that reason God banished him from paradise, because God cannot live with sin or with a sinner.

Adam at once lost the happiness he had enjoyed in paradise. His soul was darkened, his thoughts and desires were muddled, his imagination and memory began to be clouded. Instead of joy and peace of soul, he saw sorrow, afflictions, troubles, poverty, the most painful labors, and every kind of adversity; finally, sickly old age threatened him, and after that—death. But the most horrible thing of all was that the devil, who is consoled by the sufferings of men, gained power over Adam.

The very elements, that is, the air, fire, and so forth, that had previously served Adam and ministered to his pleasure, then became hostile to him. From that time, Adam and all his descendants began to feel hunger, heat, and the effects of change of winds and weather. Wild animals became savage, and began to look upon people as their enemies and as prey. From that time, people began to feel external and internal diseases that, in the course of time, increased in number and severity. Men forgot that they were brothers and began to attack one another, to hate, to deceive, to torture, and to kill. And finally, after all kinds of bitter labors and anxieties, they had to die; and as they were sinners they had to be in hell and to be eternally and unceasingly tormented there.

No human being by himself could or can restore what Adam lost. And what would have happened to us if Jesus Christ in His mercy had not redeemed us? What would have happened to the whole human race?

God, Who loves us far more than we love ourselves, in His great mercy sent us His Son Jesus Christ to save us. Jesus Christ became a man like us, but without sin.

By His teaching, Jesus Christ scattered the darkness and errors of the human mind and enlightened the whole world with the light of the Gospel. Now everyone who wants to can know the will of God and the means and way to beatitude (happiness).

By His life, Jesus Christ has shown us the way into the heavenly kingdom that Adam lost, and at the same time has shown us how we must seek it and how to follow it.

By His passion (suffering) and death, Jesus Christ has redeemed us from the debts that we had to pay to God and that we should never have been able to pay; and He has made us, who were slaves of the devil and of sin, children of God. And those torments that we, as transgressors of the will of God, would have had to suffer He bore for us. By His death He delivered us from miseries, from future torment and eternal death.

By His resurrection, Jesus Christ destroyed the gates of hell and opened to us the gates of paradise that had been closed for everyone by Adam's disobedience; and He conquered and crushed the power of the devil and death, our enemies. So now those who die in faith and hope, believing and trusting in Jesus Christ, through death pass from vain, rotten, and temporal life into a life that is bright, incorruptible, and unending; while for the conquest of the devil and for driving him away, we have the cross and prayer.

By His ascension Jesus Christ glorified the human race; for He ascended to heaven with His body which He will always have.

Finally, by the grace and merits of Jesus Christ, we can now go into the kingdom of heaven and receive support and help along the way; that is, we can all freely and truly receive the Holy Spirit and be filled with Him. Without the Holy Spirit, it is impossible to go the way Jesus Christ went.

If Jesus Christ had not been on earth, no one could have entered the kingdom of heaven. But now we all, each one of us, can easily enter it; but we cannot enter it otherwise than by the way Jesus Christ went when living on earth.

But what the Lord has prepared for us there in heaven, no one can tell or imagine. We can only say that those who believe in Jesus Christ and follow His commandments will, after their death, live with the angels, the righteous, and the saints in heaven and will see God face to face. They will rejoice with pure, constant, and eternal joy, and they will never know weariness, or sorrow, or worry, or torment, or suffering. At the end of the world, they will rise with their bodies and will reign with Christ eternally.

All these benefits Jesus Christ will give not to just one people, but to all without exception. Whoever wants to can receive them. The way has been shown, arranged, and, as far as possible, smoothed and made level. And besides that, Jesus Christ is ready to help us to go this way, and He Himself is willing to lead us by the hand, so to speak. It only remains for us not to oppose Him and not to be obstinate, but to surrender ourselves completely to His will. Let Him lead us where and how He wills.

You see how Jesus Christ loves us and what blessing He has bestowed upon us!

What would happen now if Jesus Christ suddenly appeared before us visibly and asked us, "My children, do you love Me for what I have done for you? And do you feel in your hearts gratitude to Me?" Who of us would not say: "Yea, Lord, we love and thank Thee"?

But if you love Jesus Christ and consider yourself grateful to Him, will you do what He orders you? Because whoever loves anyone, and whoever feels grateful, will do everything he can to please his benefactor. But Jesus Christ wants from you only one thing: namely, He wants you to follow Him into the kingdom of heaven.

Jesus Christ has done everything for us; cannot we do for Him the one thing He asks? Jesus Christ came down from heaven to earth to save us; for love of Him shall we not be willing to follow Him to heaven? Jesus Christ bore for us all torments and sufferings; shall we not for Jesus Christ be willing to suffer and endure a little?

Blessed and most blessed is he who follows Jesus Christ throughout his whole life, because he will certainly be there where Jesus Christ Himself lives.

Happy is he who cares and tries to imitate Jesus Christ, because he will receive help from Jesus Christ.

But unhappy is he who has no desire to follow Jesus Christ, and excuses himself by saying that it is difficult to follow Him, or he has not the strength for it, because such a person deprives himself of the grace of God and, as it were, pushes away the helping hand of Jesus Christ.

But woe to the man who opposes Jesus Christ and is obstinate and in some manner rises up against Him, because the lot of such people is in the lake of fire burning with brimstone.

## POINTS OF REFLECTION

1. Why does self-will blur the likeness of God in us?

2. "Without the Holy Spirit, it is impossible to go the way Jesus Christ went." How do we receive and keep the Holy Spirit within us?

3. "[W]hat the Lord has prepared for us there in heaven, no one can tell or imagine." How often do we contemplate the beauty and joy of life with God in eternity? If we were to do this more, how might it affect our actions here and now?

# CHAPTER 2

# How Jesus Christ Lived on Earth, and What He Suffered for Us

Everyone must obey the law of God. That law is contained in two commandments: (1) Love the Lord thy God with all thy heart, with all thy soul, with all thy mind, and with all thy strength and (2) love thy neighbor as thyself.

According to how you fulfill this law, you will receive rewards. But there is no one, and never has been, and never will be a man who could fulfill these two commandments perfectly. Only Jesus Christ fulfilled them perfectly and without any deficiency.

In this respect all the saints, and even the greatest saints, are only like lamps, whereas Jesus Christ is like the sun in all its brilliance and splendor.

And just as it is impossible for a human being to gaze at the sun and describe it, so it is impossible to describe all the virtuous works (deeds) of Jesus Christ. Therefore,

I shall tell you only briefly about His life and virtues, and only what can be seen from the Gospel.

No human being and even no angel loved God so much as Jesus Christ loved and loves Him.

Jesus Christ always prayed to God His Father, and especially He often prayed at night and in solitude.

On every feast, especially at the Passover, Jesus went to the temple in Jerusalem, which was not near the place where He lived. Every Sabbath He went to the place where the people gathered for prayer and instruction.

In all His works (deeds), Jesus Christ always glorified the name of God, and both in secret and in public gave praise to God.

All through His life Jesus Christ truly respected, obeyed, honored, and loved His Mother and Joseph His foster father and even respected the leaders and elders and paid tribute to the earthly emperor.

Jesus Christ carried out the service and work for which He came into the world fully willing, acquiescent, and conscientious—with all fervor and love.

Jesus Christ loved everyone, wished everyone well, and did good to all, and, for the true happiness of men, He did not spare His life.

Jesus Christ bore every kind of offense or insult with unspeakable meekness and love; He did not complain about His offenders, and even did not get angry with His most open enemies who slandered Him, mocked Him, and wanted to kill Him. He could have killed and destroyed with one word all His enemies and opponents, but He did not want to do that. On the contrary, He wished them all good, did good to them, prayed for them, and wept over their perdition.

To speak briefly, from His birth until His very death, Jesus Christ did not commit the smallest sin, either in word, or deed, or thought; but He did all kinds of good at all times and to all people.

Now let us look and see how Jesus Christ suffered for us here on earth. Being the Son of God and Himself God, Jesus Christ took upon Himself the body and soul of a man, and became a perfect man, without sin. Being almighty, He took the form of a slave. Being King of heaven and earth, He was born in poverty of a poor mother, in a cave, and was laid in a manger. His foster father was a poor carpenter.

Jesus Christ, the Supreme Lawgiver, to fulfill what the law required, on the eighth day after His birth shed His most precious blood through circumcision. After that, His Most-Pure Mother took Him into the temple and for Him, the Redeemer of the world, paid the redemption.[1] While Jesus Christ was still in His cradle, Herod tried to kill Him, and He fled into Egypt, a foreign country.

---

[1] By Mosaic law, the firstborn had to be redeemed by the payment of five shekels, which equals approximately ten shillings, which went into the priests' treasury (Num 18:15–17).

But do not think that Jesus Christ in His infancy could not understand what was done and what happened to Him. No! Although Jesus Christ is perfect man, yet at the same time He is also perfect God, and therefore He saw and knew everything that was done to Him.

Jesus Christ, being God and the Almighty Whom heaven and earth and myriads of angels obey, Himself throughout His earthly life obeyed His Mother Who is His Own creation.

Jesus Christ, Who has in His right hand all the treasures of the worlds, during His earthly life had no place on earth to lay His head.

Jesus Christ, the King of the whole universe, paid tribute to an earthly king.

Jesus Christ, Whom all angels and all creatures serve, Himself served men and washed the feet of His disciples who were chosen from the most uneducated and simplest of the people.

Jesus Christ suffered during His preaching a countless multitude of insults of every kind from His enemies. They called Him a sinner and a transgressor of the law of Moses, and an idle fellow, and a carpenter's son, and a friend and comrade of gluttons, wine drinkers, and tax collectors. At one time, the malice and fury of His enemies reached such a pitch that they wanted to throw Him down a mountain. On another occasion they wanted to stone Him to death. They called His most holy teaching lies and deception. When He healed the sick or raised the dead His enemies said that He did all that with the help of Satan and suggested to the people that even He Himself had a demon in Him.

In short, from His birth till His very death Jesus Christ suffered and saw sorrows and outrages on all sides. He suffered both from men and for men. He was grieved not only because people would not listen to Him and offended Him, but also because they were perishing and were unwilling to be saved from their perdition. Jesus Christ suffered, so to speak, both visibly and invisibly, because He saw and endured not only open insults and outrages from men, but at the same time He saw the secret evil thoughts and intentions of His enemies, and He saw that the very people who apparently loved and listened to Him either did not believe in Him or were indifferent to their salvation.

From whom did Jesus Christ suffer most? From the Jewish chief priests and from the scribes, that is, from the learned and from their chiefs who knew and expected the Savior's coming to them but were unwilling to receive Jesus Christ or listen to Him, but on the contrary, delivered Him to death as if He were a deceiver and lawbreaker; and when the Jewish people were ready to deliver Jesus from crucifixion, they (the priests and scribes) incited them to ask rather for the robber and rebel Barabbas, and to deliver Jesus, Who is holier than all saints, to death. To what lengths can the envy and malice of men go! But what is most horrible, Jesus Christ was betrayed by a man who was His disciple, who knew Him, who had eaten and drunk with Him, and had seen with his own eyes His life, His miracles, and the power of His teaching. And how was He betrayed? By treachery and by a kiss. And for what price? For thirty pieces of silver.

For whom did Jesus Christ suffer? For all sinners, from Adam till the end of the world. He suffered also for those very men who tortured Him, and for His enemies who had delivered Him to that torture, and for those who, having received from Him countless benefits, not only did not thank Him but even hated and persecuted Him. He also suffered for all of us who offend Him daily by our untruths, wickedness, and terrible indifference to His sufferings for us who, by our ingratitude and abominable sins, as it were, crucify Him a second time.

Toward the end of His earthly life Jesus Christ worked one of the greatest miracles, that is, He raised Lazarus who had already been four days in the grave and had begun to decompose. This miracle, which was worked in the presence of a great crowd of people, persuaded many to believe in Jesus Christ and acknowledge Him as the Messenger of God. But instead of accepting Jesus Christ and believing in Him and assuring others that He is the true Savior of the world, the Jewish chief priests and scribes gathered round Caiaphas and took counsel concerning what to do with Jesus, and they tried to find accusations against Him; and finally they decided to deliver to death Jesus Christ Who raised the dead.

But how Jesus Christ suffered on the last night, that is, after the Last Supper until His delivery into the hands of the soldiers, it is impossible for us even to imagine. His inner sufferings at that time were so great and terrible that only Jesus Christ could bear them. In Gethsemane, He sweated blood.

At that time, His soul felt cruel agony, great sorrow, and terrible suffering. His soul was covered with shame and horror at our sins which He took upon Himself, for all the sins of men committed from Adam till that time, and for the sins that will be committed till the end of the world.

Then Jesus Christ saw that even among Christians themselves there will soon appear hypocritical disciples such as Judas and that many of them not only will not imitate Him, but will give way to vices and vile and abominable sins, and even many will appear who will renounce faith itself and His teaching, or will distort them by false explanations and, instead of surrendering themselves to the wisdom of God, will themselves want to guide others according to their own ideas.

On the one hand, love for God His Father required Him to destroy the human race as ungrateful criminals, whereas on the other love for fallen and perishing men urged Him to suffer for them and by His suffering to deliver them from eternal perdition.

These sufferings were so great and grievous for Jesus Christ that He said to His disciples, "My soul is exceedingly sorrowful, even to death" (Matt 26:38; Mark 14:34).

After that, they bound Jesus Christ as if He were an evildoer and led Him away to His enemies who judged Him and condemned Him to death. The apostles, whom He had especially loved above all, forsook Him and fled. To Pilate's question, "Whom shall I release, Barabbas or Christ?" His jealous and malicious enemies incited the senseless people to ask for Barabbas the robber and to crucify Jesus the Just and Holy One. And so they delivered Him into the hands of the heathen who tortured Him, scourged Him, spat on Him, mocked Him, put on His head a crown of thorns, took His clothes off, nailed Him to a cross and crucified Him between two robbers and in a shameful place, as if He were a great malefactor and criminal. Their cruel malice and envy did not spare Him even on the cross, for even there they derided Him as a deceiver, and to quench His thirst they gave Him vinegar and gall to drink.

And at last Jesus Christ dies, and He dies by death on a cross, that is, by a painful and shameful death.

Do not think that Jesus Christ suffered because He could not have escaped or avoided the tortures. No! He gave Himself up by His own will and offered Himself as a sacrifice; otherwise no one would have dared even to think of touching Him, for you know that when those who had been sent for Him came to take Him, He asked them, "'Whom are you seeking?' They answered Him, 'Jesus of Nazareth.' Jesus said to them, "I am He'" (John 18:5–7). And at that one word, they all fell to the ground.

This is all we can say of the sufferings of Jesus Christ— that He endured for us out of His unspeakable love for us. In order to realize, as far as possible, how great is His love for us and to understand the greatness of His sacrifice, we must remember Whom Jesus Christ is. Jesus Christ is true God, the almighty Creator of the whole universe, the great King of angels and men, the powerful Lord of all creatures, the awful Judge of the living and the dead. This same Jesus Christ willed to suffer for mankind.

## POINTS OF REFLECTION

1. "Jesus Christ, the King of the whole universe, paid tribute to an earthly king." How should we show honor to those in authority in the Church and in the secular state that we live today?

2. "Jesus Christ saw that even among Christians themselves there will soon appear hypocritical disciples." Do we let what we perceive as hypocrisy in others undermine our faith? How might we prevent this?

3. How is God's love for us demonstrated by the sufferings of Jesus Christ?

CHAPTER 3

# The Way That Leads into the Kingdom of Heaven

The way into the heavenly kingdom is Jesus Christ Himself. Only those who go by this way follow Jesus Christ. But as to how we must go by this way, listen to what Jesus Christ Himself says: "If anyone desires to come after Me, let him deny himself, and take up his cross, and follow Me" (Matt 16:24). And what it means to deny oneself, take up one's cross, and follow Jesus Christ will be told in the following pages.

Jesus Christ said, "Whosoever will come after Me." These words mean that Jesus Christ does not compel or force anyone to follow Him. He does not want to have as His disciples those who are unwilling or those who have no special desire to follow Him, but wants us willingly and without any compulsion to surrender ourselves wholly to Him. Consequently, only those who desire to do so enter the kingdom of heaven. Christian, your salvation or perdition depends on your own will! In His

19

unspeakable wisdom and love, the Lord has given you freedom to do what you like, and He does not wish to take this most precious gift away from you. And so, if you wish to follow Jesus Christ, He will show you the way into the kingdom of heaven and will even help you along the way. But if you do not wish to follow Him, do as you like: No one is going to compel you or force you. But beware of despising the call of Jesus Christ and His loving kindness. In His great goodness, Christ knocks for a long, long time on the door of everyone's heart to awaken his soul and arouse in it a desire for salvation. But woe to the man whom He finally abandons and whom He casts out as a son of perdition!

And so, to follow Jesus Christ, first of all you need to have a special desire and resolve to do so; and to have a desire to follow Him, you must know where to go, and what the way is, and what is needed for this way. But how can you know what you do not want to know, or what you have only heard about slightly and superficially!?

And so, before following Jesus Christ, you must do the following:

1. You must study attentively the foundations of Christianity, that is, the actual books of Holy Scripture on which our Orthodox faith is founded. You should know where they came from, who wrote them and when, how they were preserved and have been handed down to us, why they are called *divine* and *sacred,* and

so on. But you must study the Holy Books in simplicity of heart, without any prejudice, without curiosity, impartially, and not beyond the limits of your mind; you should not try to penetrate and know what has been hidden from us by the wisdom of God. Such study of the faith is by no means opposed to faith, but, on the contrary, it is the binding duty of every Christian, when he reaches maturity, to know his faith thoroughly; because anyone who does not have a solid knowledge of his faith is cold and indifferent to it and frequently falls into either superstition or unbelief. How many Christians or, rather, how many people baptized in the name of Jesus Christ have perished and are perishing only because they have and had no desire to turn their attention to the foundations of our Orthodox faith! Whoever despises this duty will be speechless at the dread judgment. But not all people can to the same degree make a study of the faith, but each should do so according to his ability, knowledge, and enlightenment. Thus, for example, an educated person can and should direct his attention to the historical events that prove the origin and effects of the faith, to the spirit of Holy Scripture, and so on. But an uneducated and simple person should ask and learn from the pastors and teachers of the Church, because they have promised to teach the faith and have been learning from their childhood, and they consecrate all their life to the study of the faith.

2. When you know and are certain that our Orthodox faith is based on Sacred Scripture and not on fictions or speculations, and that Holy Scripture really is the Word of God revealed to us by the Holy Spirit through the prophets and apostles, then do not pry into what is hidden from us. Believe implicitly, without doubt or reservation, all that Holy Scripture teaches. Do not listen to any natural explanations and interpretations of what is beyond the human mind. And if you act in this way, your faith will be true and right, and it will be imputed to you as justification and merit.

3. Finally, try to have and to stir up within yourself a desire to do what Holy Scripture teaches. And if you have not this desire, fall at the feet of our Savior Jesus Christ and with fervent prayer implore Him to give it to you. But on no account resist when Grace calls you to the way of salvation.

All that has been said here about faith let us explain by a parable. For example, you may have heard that in a certain place near you there is a colossal, wonderful building. Its height reaches to heaven itself. The entrance to it is somewhat hidden, and without guidance not everyone can find it. Many attendants are standing by to direct you and guide you farther. These attendants are at the same time physicians for the sick and crippled and dispensers of the food needed for the journey. There are so many ladders for the ascent that nearly everyone has his own. But all the ladders are steep, narrow, and poorly lighted, so that without a guide and outside help it is impossible even to take a step, especially at the beginning. This building was the work of the wisest Architect, and it was made for the very purpose of enabling people to ascend to heaven and paradise itself.

After hearing all this, no doubt you would like to be where this building leads to. But in that case how are you going to act? Of course, first of all you must go to the building, examine it carefully, ask the attendants about everything, that is, about the building itself, its purpose, how to enter it, and so on. And the attendants will gladly tell you all that is necessary. If you are an educated person, go up to the building itself, look at it from all sides, and see whether it is built on a strong foundation and whether it can bear the actual weight of the building as well as the people who enter it. If you are very learned, then examine the materials of which it is made, find out about and investigate all that your eyes can see, and for this purpose you may even use the necessary instruments. And when you have seen and are certain that the building is sound, strong, and can fully serve its purpose, then give up all further search and leave at the doors all the instruments with which you have made your investigations, because there they will only hinder and not help. And without doubt or hesitation, enter the building itself, and go without stopping and without fearing the difficulty of the ascent, which is really difficult, especially at the beginning. The ascent to heaven is difficult, but, however, it leads straight to that to which all should aspire and which all should seek all their life. Inside this building, you will meet fellow travelers with whom you will go hand in hand, and doctors if you happen to fall and be bruised; and you will find dispensers of the food you will need for the journey; you will also find guides and directors and teachers who will tell you all that is necessary, and whom you will find and meet until you meet the Lord and Creator of the building Himself. But to reach the end of the journey more quickly and more surely, the best and most hopeful thing to do is to surrender oneself completely to the will of the Builder and Lord.

But would it not be unreasonable if someone, instead of examining the building at its very foundation and looking at what our eyes can see, out of pride and self-confidence or out of obstinacy took it into his head to examine the very top of the building that must generally be hidden in the clouds and in the vast expanse between earth and heaven? And would it not be stupid for a person who had seen certain parts of the building and had been unable to examine them properly to presume to judge them and to draw conclusions about the whole building, and to find defects or excesses where, on account of the extreme height, the building itself was scarcely visible? Or would it not be unreasonable on his part and even criminal if, without examining it at all and scarcely entering the enclosure of the building, he were suddenly to begin to criticize something or other in it and to assure others that the building was unsound and unnecessary; or instead of the laws and teachings of the Architect and Master of the house, he were to put forward his own ideas and teachings? But perhaps the most stupid of all would be the man who, when he had hardly entered the enclosure, abandoned all desire not only to enter the building but even to look at it.

For anyone who has a sincere desire to be where this building leads, it is sufficient if he is convinced that it is sound and established on a firm foundation and built not by the hands of ordinary artists and workmen, but by the hands of the great Architect Who opened the way into it and cleansed it by His blood and went by it Himself first. It is sufficient to be convinced of this; and all the rest, that is, why it is built as it is and not otherwise, or why it is there and not in another place, and so on—all this is not your business. Your business is to surrender yourself to the will of the Master of the house and with hope (trust) in His help and with love for Him in your heart to go to Him and follow Him, and to go as He orders.

Let us apply this parable to Christianity. The building built on earth and reaching to Heaven is our Orthodox Christian faith; the Architect and Master of the house is Jesus Christ; the attendants are the pastors and teachers of the Church, and so on.

Now let us look at the way by which we must follow Jesus Christ. He said, Whoever wishes to follow Me, (1) let him deny himself, (2) take up his cross, and (3) follow Me.

And so the first duty of a Christian, of a disciple and follower of Jesus Christ, is to deny oneself.

To deny oneself means to give up one's bad habits; to root out of the heart all that ties us to the world; not to cherish bad desires and thoughts; to quench and suppress bad thoughts; to avoid occasions of sin; not to do or desire anything from self-love, but to do everything out of love for God. To deny oneself means, according to the Apostle Paul, to be dead to sin and the world but alive to God.

A Christian's second duty, that is, in following after Jesus Christ, is to take up his cross.

The word *cross* means sufferings, sorrows, and adversities. There are external and internal crosses. To take up one's cross means to accept and to bear without murmuring everything unpleasant, painful, sad, difficult, and oppressive that may happen to us in our life. And therefore, whether anyone offends you, or laughs at you, or causes you weariness, sorrow, or annoyance; or you have done good to someone and, instead of thanking you, he rises up against you and even makes trouble; or you want to do good, but you are not given a chance; or some misfortune has happened, for example, either you are ill yourself, or your wife, or children; or with all your activity and untiring labors you are suffering from want and poverty, and are so hard up that you do not know how to make both ends meet; or besides that, you are in some difficulty—bear all this without malice, without murmuring, without criticism, without complaint, that is, without regarding yourself as offended and without expecting any earthly reward in return; but bear it all with love, with joy and firmness.

To take up one's cross means not only to bear crosses laid on us by others or sent by Providence, but to take and carry one's own crosses, and even to lay crosses upon oneself and bear them. This means that a Christian can and should make and keep various vows and promises that are troublesome and burdensome for one's heart; but they should be vows in conformity with the Word of God and His will, and not according to our own ideas and fancies. Thus, for example, one can and should make and keep vows useful to one's neighbors, for example, to tend the sick; to help practically those in need of help; to seek out cases; and with patience and meekness to work for the salvation and welfare of others, either by action or by word, or by advice, or by prayer, and so forth.

And if when you are bearing your cross according to the word and intention of the Lord a proud thought rises up within you, that you are not like other people but firm, pious, and better than your neighbors and companions, uproot such thoughts as far as possible, for they can destroy all your virtues.

It was said before that there are external and internal crosses, but so far we have spoken almost entirely about external crosses. And blessed is he who can bear them wisely and well, for the Lord will not let such a man perish, but He will send him the Holy Spirit Who will strengthen and guide him and lead him further. But to become holy and be like Jesus Christ, merely external crosses are not enough; for external crosses without internal ones are of no more use than external prayer without internal prayer. Outward crosses and outward sufferings are borne not only by disciples of Jesus Christ, but by all and everyone. There is not a man on earth who has not suffered in one way or another. But whoever wants to be a true disciple and follower of Jesus Christ must bear without fail internal crosses as well.

Internal crosses can be found at all times, and more easily than external ones. You have only to direct your attention to yourself and to examine your soul with a sense of penitence, and a thousand internal crosses will at once present themselves. For instance, consider: How did you come to be in this world? Why are you in this world at all? Do you live as you ought to live? And so on. Pay due attention to this, and you will see at first glance that, being the creation and work of the hands of Almighty God, you exist in this world solely, with all your actions, with all your life, and with your whole being, to glorify His holy and great Name. But you not only fail to glorify Him, but on the contrary you offend and dishonor Him by your sinful life. Then recollect and consider: What awaits you on the other side of your grave? On which side will you be at the time of Christ's dread judgment, on the left or the right? And if you reflect in this way, you will inevitably be alarmed and will begin to be disquieted. And this will be the beginning of internal crosses. But if you not only do not banish such thoughts from you, or seek diversion from them in worldly pleasures or empty amusements, but still further and more attentively examine yourself, you will find still more crosses. For example, hell, which up till now you have perhaps scarcely thought of, or have thought of with indifference, will then appear to you in all its horror. Paradise, which the Lord has prepared for you and to which you have hitherto hardly given a thought, will then become to you the living reality that it actually is, a place of pure and eternal joys of which you are depriving yourself by your carelessness and stupidity.

And if you do not pay any attention to the troubles and inner sufferings that you feel from such thoughts, and firmly resolve to bear them without seeking consolation in anything earthly, but pray more fervently to the Lord for your salvation and surrender the whole of yourself to His will, then the Lord will begin to show and reveal to you the state of your soul as it really is to introduce and nourish within you fear, affliction, and sorrow and thereby purify you more and more.

We can never see the state of our soul in all its nakedness or vividly realize its danger without the special grace and help of the Lord, because the interior of our soul is always hidden from us by our self-love, prejudices, passions, worldly cares, and delusions. And if it some-times seems to us that we see the state of our soul our-selves, yet we see it only superficially and no more than our own reason and conscience can show us.

Knowing how good for us it is to examine and see the state of our soul, the enemy of our soul (the devil) uses all his wiles and cunning to prevent us from seeing the state in which we really are, lest we should be converted and begin to seek salvation. But when the devil sees that his wiles do not help and that the man with the help and Grace of God is beginning to see himself, then the devil employs another still more crafty means—he endeavors to show a man the state of his soul suddenly and, as far as possible, more from the dangerous side, so as thereby to strike the man with terror and lead him to despair. And if the Lord were actually to allow the devil always to use this last means, that is, to show us the state of our soul from the most dangerous side, few of us would stand firm; because the state of the soul of a sinner, and especially of a sinner who has not repented, really is extremely dangerous and terrible; and not only the soul of a sinner, but even the most holy and righteous people, with all their righteous-ness, could not find tears enough to weep for their soul.

When the Lord is pleased to reveal to you the state of your soul, then you begin to see clearly and to feel acutely that with all your virtues your heart is corrupt and perverted, your soul is defiled, and you yourself are only a slave of sin and the passions that have completely mastered you and do not allow you to draw near to God. You also begin to see that there is nothing truly good in you, and even if you have some good works, they are all mixed with sin and are not the fruit of true love but are the product of various passions and circumstances; and then you will certainly suffer. You will be overwhelmed with fear, sorrow, misery, and so forth—fear because you are in danger of perishing; sorrow and misery because you have so long and so stubbornly closed your ears to the gentle voice of the Lord calling you into the heavenly kingdom and you have so long and so brazenly angered Him with your sins.

And in proportion as the Lord reveals to you the state of your soul, your internal sufferings will also increase.

Now you see what internal crosses are!

Just as not all people have the same virtues and the same sins, so internal crosses are not the same for all. For some, they are more oppressive, and for others, less; for certain people, they are more prolonged, and for others, less; for some they come in one way, and for others, quite differently. And all this depends on the state of each person's soul, just as the length and mode of cure of an illness depends on the patient's condition. It is not the doctor's fault if he must sometimes use violent and prolonged means for the cure of a chronic and dangerous illness that perhaps the sick man himself irritated and increased. Whoever wants to be well will consent to bear everything.

Internal crosses are sometimes so burdensome that the sufferer can find no consolation whatsoever in anything.

All this can happen to you too! But in whatever position you may be, and whatever sufferings of soul you may feel, do not despair and do not think that the Lord has abandoned you. No! He will always be with you and will invisibly strengthen you even when it seems to you that you are on the very brink of perdition. He will never allow you to be tempted more than He sees fit. Do not despair and do not be afraid, but with full submission and devotion to Him, have patience and pray. For He is always our Father, and a very loving Father. Even if He permits a person who has surrendered to Him to fall into temptation, yet it is only to make him realize more clearly his own impotence, weakness, and nothingness and to teach him never to trust in himself and to show that no one can do anything good without God. And if the Lord leads a person into suffering or lays crosses upon him, it is only to heal his soul, to make him like Jesus Christ, and to perfectly purify his heart, in which He Himself wishes to dwell with the Son and the Holy Spirit.

In these troubles of yours, however trying they may be, do not seek consolation among men unless the Lord specially indicates it and sends you His chosen servants. Ordinary people, that is, those who are not experienced in spiritual matters, are always bad comforters, even in ordinary sorrows, and still more in spiritual sorrows and troubles from the Lord, which they do not even understand; in this case, they are more likely to do you harm than to comfort and relieve your sufferings. The Lord Himself is your Helper and Comforter and Guide; run to Him alone, and in Him alone seek consolation and help.

Blessed, a hundred times blessed, is the person whom the Lord grants to bear internal crosses, because they are the true healing of the soul, the sure and safe way of becoming like Jesus Christ, and consequently they are a special and manifest favor of the Lord, and they show clearly His care for our salvation. Blessed is that man also because he is in a state of grace to which we not only cannot attain without the assistance of the Grace of God but do not even consider necessary for our salvation.

If you bear your sufferings with submission and surrender to the will of the Lord and do not seek consolation anywhere or in anyone except the Lord, then in His mercy He will not abandon you and will not leave you without consolation; He will touch your heart with His Grace and will communicate to you the gifts of the Holy Spirit. Amid your sufferings, and perhaps even at the very beginning of them, you will feel in your heart ineffable sweetness, a wonderful peace and joy that you never felt before, and at the same time, you will feel within you the power and ability to pray to God with true prayer and to believe in Him with true faith. Then your heart will burn with pure love for God and your neighbor. All this is a gift of the Holy Spirit.

And if the Lord grants you such a gift, whatever you do, do not regard it as a reward for your labors and troubles, and do not think that you have attained perfection or sanctity. Such thoughts are inspired by pride that has so deeply penetrated our soul and has taken root so strongly in us that it can make its appearance even when a person has miracle-working power.

These consolations and touches of the Holy Spirit are not a reward, but only the mercy of the Lord Who grants you to taste the good things that He has prepared for those who love Him, so that having tasted them you may seek them with greater zeal and fervor, and at the same time may prepare and strengthen yourself to endure fresh troubles and sufferings. And the love that you feel at that time is not the perfect state to which the saints attain on earth, but only an indication of it.

The third duty of the disciple of Jesus Christ is to follow Him. To follow Jesus Christ means to imitate in all our works and acts the works and acts of Jesus Christ. Just as Jesus Christ lived and acted on earth, so we should also live and act. For example, Jesus Christ always gave thanks and praise to God His Father, and always prayed to Him. So too in every state and in all the circumstances of our life we should thank God, love Him, and both publicly and privately give praise to Him, pray to Him, and always have Him in our minds and hearts.

Jesus Christ honored His immaculate Mother and His foster father and superiors and obeyed them. In exactly the same way, we, too, should honor and obey our parents and teachers and not irritate or grieve them by our behavior, and we should respect our superiors and all authorities (called of God), and we should submit to them and obey them without a murmur.

Jesus Christ, the universal King, paid tribute (tax) to the earthly king, and the Judge of the living and dead was unwilling to take upon Himself the civil authority of a judge or arbitrator (Luke 12:14). Just so, we ought to pay the taxes to our king without any murmuring, and we ought not to take upon ourselves any authority that does not belong to us, for example, the authority of a judge, and condemn (or criticize) those in authority.

Jesus Christ fulfilled the duty He undertook and the work for which He was sent into the world willingly and with zeal and love. In exactly the same way, we too should carry out such duties as are assigned to us by God and the king (or government) conscientiously, willingly, and without murmuring, even though our duties may be difficult or menial.

Jesus Christ loved everyone, and did every kind of good to all. So we too should love our neighbors and, as far as possible, do good to them by deed, or word, or thought.

Jesus Christ gave Himself up for the salvation of men. So too, in order to do good to people, we should not spare our labors or help. For the salvation and defense of our king and country (the king being the father of the nation), we should not spare even our life itself; whereas for Jesus Christ, as our Redeemer and Benefactor, we should not spare the very comforts of our soul, nor our body, nor our life, as did the holy martyrs who suffered various tortures and death for Jesus Christ.

Jesus Christ willingly surrendered Himself to suffering and death. So, too, should we not avoid the sufferings and sorrows sent us by God but ought to accept and bear them with humility and surrender to God.

Jesus Christ forgave His enemies all that they did to Him, and, over and above that, He did them every kind of good and prayed for their salvation. So too should we forgive our enemies, repay with good the evil done us, and bless those who curse and abuse us, with full faith and hope in God, the most just and all-seeing Judge, without Whose will not even a hair of our head will be lost. By bearing wrongs without complaint, without revenge, and with love, you will act as a true Christian (Matt 5:44; Luke 6:28).

Jesus Christ, the King of heaven and earth, lived in poverty and earned His living by His own labors. So too should we be industrious and have a love of work, and seek without laziness what is necessary for our life, and be content with our state and not desire wealth; because, according to the Savior's word, it is easier for a camel to go through the eye of a needle than for a rich man to enter the kingdom of heaven.

Jesus Christ, being meek and humble in heart, never sought or desired praise from others. So too should we never boast or pride ourselves on anything at all or seek praise from others. For instance, if you do good to others, if you give alms, if you live more piously than others, or if you are more intelligent than many, or in general if you are better and more distinguished than your fellows, do not be proud of it either before men or to yourself, because all that you have that is good and praiseworthy is not yours but the gift of God—only sins and weaknesses are your own, and all the rest is God's.

To follow Jesus Christ means also to obey the word of Jesus Christ. Therefore, we must listen to, believe, and fulfill all that Jesus Christ has said in the Gospel and through His apostles, and we must do all this without philosophizing and in simplicity of heart. He who listens and attends to the word of Jesus Christ may be called His disciple; but he who listens to and carries out His word and will with simplicity of heart and with perfect devotion is His true, beloved disciple.

And so, that is what it means to deny oneself, to take up one's cross and follow Jesus Christ. That is the true nature and property of a disciple of Jesus Christ. That is the true and straight way into the kingdom of heaven. And that is the way by which Jesus Christ Himself went while He lived on earth, and by which we Christians must go. There never was, and is not, and never will be any other way.

Certainly this way is rough, narrow, and thorny, and it seems so especially at the beginning. But it leads straight to paradise, to the heavenly kingdom, to eternal beatitude, to God Who is the source of all beatitude. Sorrowful is this way, yet for every step we take along it, thousands of rewards lie ahead. The sufferings on this way are not eternal, and one can say that they are even no more than momentary, whereas the rewards for them are unending and eternal, as is God Himself. The sufferings will become less and lighter from day to day, while the reward will increase from hour to hour, throughout an infinite eternity.

And so, do not be afraid of this way, for the smooth and easy way leads to hell, and the rough and thorny way leads to heaven.

Many ask in perplexity, "Why is the way to the heavenly kingdom so difficult?" and "Why must a Christian bear such heavy crosses?" To these and similar questions, the Christian should always reply that so it is pleasing to God. Our God is all wise and the lover of mankind; He knows what He is doing, and what to do with us. If we really wish to be true disciples of Jesus Christ, that is, disciples who are submissive, obedient, and devoted to Him, let us surrender ourselves and each other and all our life to Christ our God. But it is possible to show a few plain and comprehensible reasons why the way into the kingdom of heaven is so difficult and that we cannot possibly avoid it if we wish to attain salvation.

1. The kingdom of heaven is the very highest beatitude, and the greatest glory and honor, and the most

inexhaustible riches, and therefore if great cares and labors are necessary to obtain a trifling quantity of earthly wealth, how can such an unspeakable treasure be obtained without labors?

2. The kingdom of heaven is a reward, and the very greatest reward; and where is a reward given free and for nothing? So, if it is necessary to labor and struggle to get an earthly and temporal reward, how much more must it be necessary to get a heavenly and eternal reward?

3. We must bear crosses because we call ourselves and wish to be Christians, that is, disciples, followers, and members of Jesus Christ. Whatever the Master, Leader, and Head is like, so ought also His disciples, followers, and members be. Jesus Christ entered into His glory through sufferings; consequently, we too can enter there only by the way of sufferings.

4. All carry their crosses; all have to suffer. To carry the cross is not the portion or lot only of Christians. No! Both the Christian and the non-Christian, the believer and the unbeliever, carry the cross. The only difference is that for the one the cross serves as a cure and as a means of inheriting the kingdom of heaven, whereas for the other it becomes a chastisement, penalty, and punishment. For the one, crosses gradually become lighter and sweeter and are finally turned into crowns of eternal glory, whereas for the other they become heavier and more grievous, and in the end all

the crosses of the world will converge into one great hellish burden that will weigh down upon their heads and beneath which they will suffer eternally and without respite. But what is the cause of such a difference? The reason is that the one carries them with faith and surrender to God, and the other with murmuring and blasphemies. And so, Christian, you should not only not avoid crosses and not murmur at them, but, on the contrary, you should thank Jesus Christ for sending them to you, and thank Him day and night for granting you to be numbered among His crusaders or cross bearers. For if Jesus Christ had not suffered for the world, not one of us would ever have entered the kingdom of heaven, however much we may have suffered and been tortured; because then we should have had to suffer as condemned and rejected violators of the will of God, and we should have had to suffer without hope or consolation. But now, although we suffer, we suffer or can suffer for salvation, for deliverance, with hope, with consolation, and so as to receive a reward. O merciful Lord, how great is Thy love for us! O Jesus Christ, how great are Thy benefits to us! Thou turnest the very evil of the world into a blessing for us, to our profit and for our salvation. Christian! Gratitude and love for Jesus Christ, your Benefactor, alone obliges you to follow Him. Jesus Christ came down to earth for you; will you grudge Him anything earthly? Jesus Christ drank for you and for your sake the full chalice of sufferings; will you not swallow one drop of bitterness for Him?

5. Jesus Christ redeemed us by His passion and death; and therefore by right of redemption we belong to Him. Consequently, we are not our own, but His; therefore we must carry out and do all that He orders, if we do not wish to be cast away from His presence. But Jesus Christ demands of us only one thing, and even that for our own welfare—that we follow Him into the heavenly kingdom.

6. Jesus Christ did not suffer and die to give us the will to do all that we want. No, God preserve us from thinking so!

7. Finally, let us say why we cannot possibly avoid the narrow way into the kingdom of heaven: (a) Because in every man there is sin, and sin is a wound that does not heal by itself, without medicines, and in the case of some people, this wound is so deep and dangerous that it can be healed only by cauterization and amputation; that is why no one can be cleansed of his sins without spiritual sufferings; and (b) sin is the most horrible impurity and abomination in the eyes of God; but nothing abominable, vile, and unclean can enter the kingdom of heaven. Wherever you put a person suffering from an internal disease or oppressed with cruel sorrow, he will suffer, even if he is put in the most magnificent palace; that is because his disease and sorrow are always and everywhere with him and in him.

It is the same in the case of a sinner who is impenitent and not cleansed of his sins—wherever you put him, he will suffer, even in paradise itself, because the cause of his suffering (i.e., sin) is in his heart. To a sinner, everywhere will be hell. However, whoever feels real, heartfelt joy will rejoice both in a palace and in a hut, and even in prison, because his joy is in his heart. So too for a righteous man whose heart is filled with consolations of the Holy Spirit; wherever he may be, everywhere will be paradise because the kingdom of heaven is within us (Luke 17:21). However much you cut off the branches of a living tree, it will not die, but will again produce new branches, and to destroy it completely you must tear it out of the ground by its roots. In exactly the same way, you cannot destroy sin from the human heart by lopping off or giving up a few vices or habits; and therefore whoever wishes to destroy sin from the heart must tear out the actual root of sin. But the root of sin is deeply embedded in the human heart and firmly attached to it, and therefore it is quite impossible to eradicate it without pain. And unless the Lord had sent us the Great Physician, Jesus Christ, no one could have destroyed the root of sin, and all efforts and attempts to do so would have proved absolutely futile.

And so, brethren, you see that we must follow Jesus Christ without fail and that we cannot possibly avoid the way by which Jesus Christ went. Also, you see that without suffering no one can enter the kingdom of heaven, because all the saints and servants of God went by this same way. Some say, "How can we who are so weak and sinful be like the saints, and how are we to be saved? We live in the world and have various duties." Oh, brethren! This is not only untrue, but it is blasphemy and an insult to our Creator. To excuse yourself with pretexts of this kind means to accuse our Creator of being incompetent in creating us. No, this is an empty and blasphemous excuse, and not a reason. Look at the saints! They were not all hermits; and they were like us at first and were not sinless, and they were also engaged in worldly affairs, cares, and duties, and many of them had a family as well. But while doing their worldly occupations and duties, at the same time they did not forget their duties as Christians; and while living in the world, at the same time they made their way into the kingdom of heaven, and often led others with them as well. In exactly the same way, if we wish, we can be at once good citizens, faithful husbands, and good fathers, and also good and faithful Christians. True Christianity is never and nowhere a hindrance, but, on the contrary, is everywhere and for everything beneficial. A true Christian is only a person who believes in Jesus Christ and imitates Him in everything. The spirit of Christianity is pure, disinterested, spiritual love, love that is a gift of the Holy Spirit (many things are called love by people, but not all are Christian love).

So, brethren, if you wish to be in the kingdom of heaven, you must go the way Jesus Christ went; otherwise you will be lost, and lost for ever.

But here it is necessary to say that anyone going the Christian way who trusts in his own powers will not be able to take even a single step forward. And if Jesus Christ, our great Benefactor, had not given us help, no one could have gone this way. Even the apostles themselves, when they were without this help, could not do anything—they were afraid and terrified to follow Jesus Christ. But when they received help from Jesus Christ, they followed Him joyfully and gladly, and no difficulties or sufferings, not even death itself, could daunt them.

But what is the help that Jesus Christ gives to those who follow Him? This help is the assistance of the Holy Spirit, Whom Jesus Christ gives us, and Who is always with us and always surrounds us and draws us to Himself. And anyone who wishes can receive Him and be filled with Him. As to how the Holy Spirit helps us, and how we can receive Him, we shall see in what follows.

## POINTS OF REFLECTION

1. What are the "foundations of Christianity"? How well do we know them and how might we become more familiar with them?

2. "[T]he first duty of a Christian, of a disciple and follower of Jesus Christ, is to deny oneself." How do we do this according to St Innocent?

3. What does it mean to take up our cross in following Christ?

4. What is an "internal cross"?

5. What does it mean to "follow Jesus Christ"? Give practical examples.

6. "Both the Christian and the non-Christian, the believer and the unbeliever, carry the cross." Explain this statement.

# CHAPTER 4

# How Jesus Christ Helps Us to Go the Way into the Kingdom of Heaven, and How We Can Receive His Help

The Holy Spirit, as God, the third Person of the Holy Trinity, is also almighty, like the Father and the Son. He vivifies, animates, and gives creatures their powers. He gives animals their life, men their mind, and Christians their high spiritual life: that is, the Holy Spirit enlightens man and helps him to enter the kingdom of heaven.

The Holy Spirit is not given according to our merits but is a free gift sent by the mercy of God for the salvation of men. The Holy Spirit assists us in these ways:

1. When the Holy Spirit comes to dwell in a man, He gives him faith and light. Without Him no one can have true, living faith. Without the illumination of the Holy Spirit, the wisest and most learned man is completely blind as regards the works and ways of God. However, the Holy Spirit can reveal Himself to the simplest and most illiterate person internally,

and directly show him the works of God, and cause him to feel the sweetness of the heavenly kingdom. A person who has within him the Holy Spirit feels in his soul an extraordinary light, previously quite unknown to him.

2. When the Holy Spirit comes to dwell in a man, He produces true love in his heart. True love in the heart is like a pure fire or warmth that sets a person aglow; it is the root that produces within him all good works. For a person animated by true love, there is nothing difficult, terrifying, or impossible; for him no laws or commandments are hard, and all are practicable. Faith and love, which are gifts of the Holy Spirit, are such great and powerful means that a person who has them can easily, and with joy and consolation, go the way Jesus Christ went.

3. Besides this, the Holy Spirit gives man the power to resist the delusions of the world, so that although he makes use of earthly goods, yet he uses them as a temporary visitor, without attaching his heart to them. But a man who has not got the Holy Spirit, despite all his learning and prudence, is always more or less a slave and worshipper of the world.

4. The Holy Spirit gives a man wisdom. This we can see especially in the case of the holy apostles who, until they had received the Holy Spirit, were simple and unlearned men, but afterward, who could resist their wisdom and the power of their word? The Holy

Spirit also gives wisdom in works and acts. Thus, a person who has the Holy Spirit always finds means and time for his salvation, and amid the turmoil of the world and in spite of all his occupations, he can enter into himself when it seems impossible to an ordinary man even in the temple of God.

5. The Holy Spirit gives true joy and gladness of heart and imperturbable peace. A person who has not the Holy Spirit can never rejoice with true joy and be glad with pure gladness, and he cannot have that peace of soul that makes life sweet. True, he does sometimes rejoice and is glad, but what kind of joy is it? It is fleeting and impure, and his gladness is always hollow and feeble, and after it he is still more overwhelmed with boredom. And it is also true that such a person is sometimes calm, but this calmness is not peace of soul—it is a sleep or lethargy of the soul. Woe to the person who is listless and who has no desire to awake from such a sleep (Rom 13:11; Eph 5:14; 1 Cor 15:34).

6. The Holy Spirit gives true humility. Even the most intelligent person, if he has not the Holy Spirit, cannot know himself properly. Without God's help, he cannot see the inner state of his soul. If he does good to others and acts honestly, he thinks that he is a righteous man and even perfect in comparison with others, and therefore he feels that he does not need anything. Oh, how often people perish from a false assurance of their honesty and righteousness!

They perish because they trust in their own goodness and do not think about the spirit of Christianity at all or the help of the Holy Spirit, just when they are in extreme need of His help. And because the Holy Spirit is given only to those who ask and seek, and such people not only fail to ask and seek Him but do not even consider it necessary, therefore He is not given to them and, consequently, they remain in error and perish. But when the Holy Spirit dwells in the heart of a person, He shows him all his inner poverty and weakness, and the corruption of his heart and soul, and his separation from God, and with all his virtues and righteousness, He shows him his sins, his sloth and indifference regarding the salvation and good of people, his self-seeking in his apparently most selfless virtues, his coarse selfishness even where he does not suspect it. To be brief, the Holy Spirit shows him everything as it really is. Then a person begins to have true humility, begins to lose hope in his own powers and virtues, and regards himself as the worst of men. And when a person humbles himself before Jesus Christ, Who alone is holy in the glory of God the Father, he begins to repent truly and resolves never again to sin but to live more carefully. And if he really has some virtues, then he sees clearly that he practiced and practices them only with the help of God, and therefore he begins to put his trust only in God.

7. The Holy Spirit teaches true prayer. No one, until he receives the Holy Spirit, can pray in a manner truly pleasing to God, because if anyone who does not have the Holy Spirit begins to pray, his soul is distracted in different directions from one thing to another, and he cannot fix his thoughts on any one thing. Moreover, he does not know properly either himself or his own need, or how to ask or what to ask of God; in fact he does not even know what God is like. But a person in whom the Holy Spirit dwells knows God and sees that He is his Father and knows how to approach Him, and how to ask and what to ask of Him. His thoughts during prayer are orderly, pure, and aspire to a single object—God. And by prayer he can do literally anything, and can even move mountains from place to place.

This is a short account of what the Holy Spirit gives to those who have Him within them! And you see that without the help and assistance of the Holy Spirit, it is impossible not only to enter the kingdom of heaven but even to take a single step toward it. And therefore we must seek and ask for the Holy Spirit and have Him within us, just as the holy apostles had Him. But how we can receive or obtain Him, we shall soon see.

Jesus Christ said that "the wind blows where it wishes, and you hear the sound of it, but cannot tell where it comes from and where it goes" (John 3:8). These words mean that we can hear, feel, and perceive the presence of the Holy Spirit in our heart or His touch upon our heart, but that we cannot tell when or how He will visit us.

We also see that the holy apostles received the Holy Spirit from Jesus Christ, and received Him frequently and at a time neither foreseen nor fixed nor arranged by them, but at the time that was pleasing to Jesus Christ. Only the solemn descent of the Holy Spirit was foretold to them, which followed at the appointed time and in the appointed place. But even then they did not receive Him for any personal merits of their own, but as a free gift, through faith and hope. And the united prayer in which they continued after the Lord's ascension until the descent of the Holy Spirit was not so much a means of receiving the Holy Spirit as a preparation for it. Consequently, no one can say definitely how or when you will receive the Holy Spirit. The Holy Spirit is the gift of God, and gifts are given unexpectedly when it is pleasing to the Dispenser of the gifts, and He distributes them to whom He wills. Therefore, those who think that they will receive the Holy Spirit in some special manner at some special time are very mistaken, and those who invent their own means of obtaining Him not only will not receive the Holy Spirit, but also take upon themselves a terrible sin.

But before speaking of how we can receive the Holy Spirit, it is necessary to say that only a true believer can receive the Holy Spirit, that is, a person who confesses the holy Orthodox Catholic faith, and who confesses it aright, without any addition, diminution, or change, but as the holy apostles delivered it to us, and as it was defined and confirmed by the Holy Fathers in the ecumenical councils. All doubt and criticism of the faith is disobedience, and an unsubmissive soul cannot be a temple or house of the Holy Spirit.

The true and recognized means of receiving the Holy Spirit, according to the teaching of Holy Scripture and the experiences of great saints, are the following: (1) purity of heart and chastity, (2) humility, (3) listening to the voice of God, (4) prayer, (5) daily self-denial, (6) reading and listening to Holy Scripture, and (7) the sacraments of the Church, and especially Holy Communion.

Every faithful soul is filled with the Holy Spirit, if she is cleansed of her sins and not encumbered or closed by self-love and pride. For the Holy Spirit always surrounds us and wishes to fill us, but our evil deeds that surround us like a hard stone wall are like evil guards that do not allow Him to come near us and keep Him away from us. Every sin can keep the Holy Spirit away from us, but bodily impurity and spiritual pride are especially repellent to Him. The Holy Spirit, Who is the most perfect purity, cannot possibly be in a man defiled by sins. How can He be in our heart when it is filled and encumbered by different cares, desires, and passions?

**PURITY**
Therefore, if we do not want to lose the Holy Spirit Whom we receive in our baptism, or if we wish to receive

Him again, then we must be pure in our hearts and must guard our bodies from unchastity, because our heart and body should be the temple of the Holy Spirit. And if a person is pure in heart and chaste in body, then the Holy Spirit enters into him and possesses his heart and soul (if only the person does not trust in his own good works and boast of them or consider that he has a right to receive the gifts of the Holy Spirit, to receive them as a due reward).

But if, unfortunately, you have defiled and corrupted your heart and body, try to cleanse yourself by repentance; that is, stop sinning and, in contrition of heart, repent that you have hitherto offended God, your most loving Father; repent and begin to live with great vigilance, and then even you will be able to receive the Holy Spirit.

## HUMILITY

One of the safest means of receiving the Holy Spirit is humility. Even though you are an honest, good, just, and merciful man, in a word, even though you have fulfilled all the commandments of God, always regard yourself as an unprofitable servant and no more than God's instrument through whom He acts. In fact, if we examine our good works more attentively, and even our greatest virtues, will many of them prove to deserve to be called Christian virtues? For example, how often do we give alms or material help to our brethren from vainglory or self-love like Pharisees, or from self-interest like moneylenders; that is, hoping in return for a nickel given to a beggar to receive from God hundreds and thousands! Certainly a good deed always remains a good deed, so continue to do and increase your good deeds. Every good deed can be called gold, and gold even when unpurified has value; it only has to be put into the hands of a master, and it will receive its true value. In the same way, your good deeds will receive their value if with full trust you commit them to the will and hands of the Great Artist. Continue to be honest, good, just, and merciful and a faithful doer of the law. But if you wish your virtues to have their real value, do not boast of them and do not regard them as pure gold that deserves heavenly treasures. You are not a master, and you cannot value them. Art gives to gold its true value, and love gives true value to the virtues— but Christian love, pure, disinterested love, that only the Holy Spirit gives. Everything that is done not according to Christian love, that is to say, without the Holy Spirit, is not true virtue. And therefore a man who has not the Holy Spirit within him, for all his virtues, is poor and indigent.

There is also another aspect of humility, that is, to bear all the troubles, sorrows, and adversities you meet with patience and without murmuring and regard them as a punishment for your sins, and do not say, "Oh, how unfortunate I am!" but say, "This is much less than I deserve for my sins!" And ask God not so much to deliver you from adversities but rather to give you the strength to bear them.

## ATTENTIVENESS

The Holy Spirit can also be received by attentively listening to the voice of God. The voice of God, Who speaks clearly, distinctly, and intelligibly, can be heard everywhere and in everything, only you need to have ears to hear. God, as your most loving Father, from your very birth daily speaks to you, calls you to Himself, warns, guides, teaches, and enlightens you. For instance, are you unhappy, has someone offended you, has one of your family died, are you ill yourself, or sad, or miserable without any apparent reason (which often happens with everyone)—in all this you can hear the voice of God speaking to you so that you should recover your senses and, instead of hoping in men and seeking help or consolation in diversions and amusements, that you should turn in penitence to God and seek comfort and help in Him alone. Or let us suppose that you are prospering, that is, that you are living in plenty and abundance; all your affairs and circumstances are in the very best state, and you do not feel sorrow and grief, but frequently feel joy, and sometimes even spiritual joy. All this is the voice of God speaking to you, so that you should love God Who is so good to you with all your heart and thank Him according to your strength, and so that while making use of the goods of this world you should not forget to gladden even the least of Jesus Christ's brothers, the poor; and that you should not forget the true goods and joys of heaven, and Him Who is the Source of all goods and joys. Who of us has not heard and does not hear the voice of God speaking through various occurrences, adventures, or events? In fact, we all hear, and hear clearly and distinctly, but not many of us understand and act according to the voice of God. Usually in our sorrows and grief, instead of entering more deeply into ourselves, we seek distraction in worldly occupations or amusements; and instead of receiving these visitations of God as a great cure and making use of them for the good of our soul, we seek deliverance from them, and sometimes even murmur and lose patience. Or at least, instead of seeking consolation in God, the Source of all consolation, we seek it in the world and its pleasures. And when we thrive and prosper, instead of loving God more and more as our Benefactor, we forget Him; and instead of using the good things that the Lord gives us for the common good and for the help of our needy brethren, we use them for our own whims and for the satisfaction of our own quite useless desires. If it is criminal and terrible to be inattentive and not listen to the voice of an earthly king, how much more sinful and terrible is it not to attend and listen to the voice of the Heavenly King. Such neglect and inattention, after His countless and constant beckoning and calls, may lead to God's finally abandoning us as obstinate children and allowing us to do whatever we like. Then little by little our mind may get darkened until the most vile and abominable sins seem to us nothing more than the unavoidable weaknesses of human nature. And therefore, just as it is profitable and salutary (saving) to be attentive to the voice of God, so too it is fatal and terrible not to listen to it and to turn away from it (Heb 12:25, 12:3, 12:7).

## PRAYER

The Holy Spirit can be received by prayer. This is the simplest and surest means, and one that everyone can always use. It is well known that prayer can be outward and inward; that is, whoever prays and bows with his body either at home or in church prays externally, whereas whoever turns to God with his heart and soul, and tries to have Him always in his mind, prays internally. Which of these prayers is better, more effectual, and more pleasing to God, everyone of you knows. You also know that you can pray to God at any time and in any place and even when sin overwhelms you. You can pray at work and without work, on a feast and on an ordinary day, standing, sitting, and lying down. You know all that. But here it needs to be said that although internal prayer is the most powerful means of receiving the Grace of God, yet we must not give up external prayer either, and especially common prayer. Many say, "Why should I go to church? I can pray at home just as well. There (at church) one sins more than prays." But what do you think makes people speak like that? Do you think it is justice or prudence? Certainly not! It is laziness and pride that makes them speak in that way. Of course, sometimes it happens, unfortunately, that just when you are in church you sin.

But that is not because you went to church, but because you did not go to church in the right spirit and you stand in church not to pray but to do something quite different. And look at those who do not go to church for the said reasons. Do they pray at home? Not at all! And even if some do pray, in the case of most of them their prayer is pharisaic, for all their prayers can be expressed by the very words the Pharisee used: "God, I thank You that I am not like other men—extortioners, unjust, adulterers" (Luke 18:11). So, go and take part in the common prayers of the Church, and pray at home before the holy icons, and pay no attention to the reasoning of the rationalists.

It was said above that a person who has not the Holy Spirit within him cannot pray true prayer. This is perfectly true. We need to make considerable use of toil and suffering to be able to pray holy prayer. We cannot suddenly or quickly attain such a state as to be able to raise our thoughts and hearts to God. Not only with us ordinary people, but even with many who have consecrated their whole life to prayer, it happens that you go to turn your thoughts to God and you find them distracted in different directions and taken up with various matters; you want to have God in your thoughts, and something quite different comes to you, and sometimes it is even something terrible.

True prayer brings with it a sweet consolation of heart, so that many holy fathers stood for whole days and nights in prayer, and in their sweet rapture they did not notice the time or the length of their prayer. For them, prayer was not a labor but a pleasure. But it is not easy to reach such a state, especially for anyone who from childhood has given free rein to his passions and stifled his conscience. But what in the world, what science or art, or what consolations are acquired by us easily, quickly, and without toil? And, therefore, pray, in spite of the fact that you do not experience in prayer any consolation or pleasure but only toil—pray, and pray diligently with all possible fervor, train yourself in prayer and in conversation with God; try as far as possible to collect and control your wandering thoughts, and little by little you will feel that it is becoming easier and easier for you, and then you will experience delightful consolations. If you are sincerely in earnest, the Holy Spirit, seeing your efforts and the sincerity of your desire, will soon help you, and then He will enter within you and will teach you to pray true prayer.

It is easiest to pray in our troubles and adversities; so do not miss such opportunities, but make use of them to pour out your sorrow before God in prayer.

Jesus Christ orders us to pray without ceasing. Many say, "How can we pray without ceasing when we are living in the world? If we spend all our time praying, when shall we do our work and attend to our business?" Of course we cannot pray without ceasing outwardly; that is, we cannot always be standing at prayer, because we must do other duties as well, and work. But whoever feels his inner poverty will not cease to pray even amid his occupations; whoever has an ardent desire to enter the kingdom of heaven will find time and occasions to pray both internally and externally. A fervent soul will find time to say a word to God and worship Him even amid the hardest and most exacting kinds of work. Only those who have no desire to pray can find no time to pray.

It is also said that God does not listen to sinners; that is, sinners do not receive from God what they ask. That is true. But to what kind of sinners is it that God does not listen? God does not hear those who pray to Him but do not think of their conversion, or those who ask God to forgive them their sins but do not want to forgive others for anything. Certainly God does not listen to such sinners and will not answer their prayers. And so when you pray to God for the forgiveness of your debts, forgive the debts of others yourself, and have a resolution to abandon your sins. If you want God to be merciful to you, be merciful to others, and then God will listen to you.

Some think that it is possible to pray only by the books. Certainly it is good if you are able to pray and glorify God in psalms and spiritual songs. But if you are illiterate, it is enough for you to know the most important prayers, and especially the Lord's Prayer (i.e., "Our Father"), because in this prayer, given us by Jesus Christ Himself, all our needs are expressed. And when circumstances do not allow you to pray longer, then say the ordinary prayers, such as "Lord have mercy!" or "God, help me!" or

"O Lord, blot out my sins!" or "Lord Jesus Christ, Son of God, have mercy on me, a sinner!"

## FASTING

One of the holy fathers said, if you want your prayer to fly up to God, then give it two wings, that is, fasting and almsgiving.

Before speaking of what fasting is let us see why fasting has been appointed. The end and purpose of fasting is to quiet and relieve the body, and so to make it more obedient to the soul, because a full and well-fed body requires luxury and rest, and disposes one to indolence, and prevents one from thinking about God; it, as it were, binds and oppresses the soul and is then like a self-willed, spoiled, and capricious wife who lords it over her husband. And now, what is fasting? Fasting varies greatly. For a person brought up in luxury, fasting can be one thing, whereas for a person brought up in simple and rough conditions, it is another thing. Therefore for one person, it is nothing to use the roughest food and be healthy, or to live without food for a number of days, whereas for another, a big change of food can be very noticeable, and even harmful. But for everyone in general fasting is above all temperance and strict moderation in the use of food. Consequently, you should use food in moderation, and try especially to bridle the desires of the body, and not satisfy its lusts at all, for they are unnecessary for the preservation of health and the prolongation of life; and then your fast will be true.

But while fasting physically, it is necessary at the same time to fast spiritually as well, that is, to restrain your tongue from evil and not speak ill of anyone or talk needlessly, to moderate your desires and root out your passions. Thus, for example, do not do today that unbecoming or unnecessary thing that you had thought of doing; tomorrow, if circumstances dispose you to be angry with anyone, calm yourself and control your heart and tongue; the day after tomorrow, if you have a desire to go to some amusement or entertainment, and especially if it is one where you may see or hear something bad, do not go there. And in this manner continue to overcome yourself. After this, begin to control and order your thoughts so that they do not wander where there is absolutely no need, because thoughts are the cause of much evil. There is nothing more difficult than to stop one's thoughts and bring them under control; in fact, it is impossible all of a sudden to order and purify one's thoughts, just as it is impossible suddenly to break and tame horses that have been running wild for a long time and have never known a bridle. In the same way, it is quite impossible for a person who has given his will and desires freedom and let them run wild all his life to reduce them suddenly to order. And moreover, when you live like an ordinary man engaged only with your worldly duties and little thinking of your duties as a Christian, then it seems to you that your thoughts are in order and even pure. But as soon as you begin to think and care about your salvation, your thoughts will at once become fuddled, just as ditch water that has stood for some time seems bright and clean as long as you do not touch it, but the more you clean out the ditch, the muddier the water becomes. It is the same with our thoughts; and finally the devil himself will stir them up. But in spite of all this, struggle with your thoughts, be strong and courageous, and never despair and think that it is quite impossible to still and purify one's thoughts. However, as far as you can, struggle and ask God for help. And the Holy Spirit, seeing your sincere desire, will dwell in you and help you.

What is almsgiving? By *almsgiving,* we usually mean giving to the poor. But under the term *almsgiving* we should understand all acts of kindness and mercy, such as feeding the hungry, giving drink to the thirsty, clothing the naked, visiting the sick and those in prison, and helping them and also giving hospitality to the homeless, looking after orphans, and so forth. But so that your almsgiving may be true, all this must be done without boasting, and without desiring praise from people for your benefactions, or gratitude from the poor. If you do as Jesus Christ Himself says, that is, "Do not let your left hand know what your right hand is doing" (Matt 6:3), then the heavenly Father Who sees in secret will reward you openly.

**SCRIPTURE**
The Holy Spirit may be received by reading and listening to Holy Scripture as the true Word of God. Holy

Scripture is a great treasury from which we can draw both light and life—light to enlighten and inform every man and life to quicken, comfort, and delight everyone. Holy Scripture is one of the greatest of God's blessings to man, and it is a blessing that can be enjoyed and used by anyone who wishes to do so. And it needs to be said that Holy Scripture is divine wisdom, and wisdom so wonderful that it can be understood and comprehended by the simplest and most unlearned person; that is why many simple people, by reading or listening to Holy Scripture, have become pious and have received the Holy Spirit. But there have also been people, and even educated people, who read Holy Scripture and erred and were lost. This is because the former read it in simplicity of heart without sophistry and rationalization and did not seek learning in it, but grace, power, and spirit, whereas the latter, on the contrary, regarding themselves as people who were wise and knew everything, sought in it not the power and spirit of the word of God, but worldly wisdom, and instead of humbly receiving all that Providence was pleased to reveal to them, they tried to discover and learn what has been hidden; and that is why they fell into unbelief or schism. It is easier to pour the whole sea into a tiny cup than for a man to comprehend all the wisdom of God.

And so, when you read or listen to Holy Scripture, lay aside all your human wisdom and submit yourself to the word and will of Him Who speaks to you through Holy Scripture, and ask Jesus Christ to instruct you Himself, to

enlighten your mind and give you a desire to read Holy
Scripture and do what it says.

There are many books in the world called profitable
and soul saving, but only those are really worthy of this
description that are based on Holy Scripture and that are
in agreement with the teaching of our Orthodox Church.
Such books can and should be read, but in choosing them
you need to be careful, lest what seems to be a salutary
book should turn out to be one that can ruin your soul.

## SACRAMENT

Jesus Christ said, "He who eats My flesh and drinks My
blood abides in Me, and I in him"; he "has eternal life,
and I will raise him up at the last day" (John 6:56, 6:54).
That means that he who worthily partakes of the holy
sacrament is mystically united to Jesus Christ. In other
words, whoever receives the Body and Blood of Christ
with true repentance, with a clean soul, with the fear of
God, and with faith at the same time receives the Holy
Spirit Who enters the soul and prepares a place there for
the reception of Jesus Christ Himself and God the Father,
and consequently the person becomes a temple and habi-
tation of the living God. But he who partakes of the Body
and Blood of Christ unworthily, that is, with an unclean
soul, with a heart full of malice, revenge, and hatred, not
only will not receive the Holy Spirit but will become like
the traitor Judas, and, as it were, crucifies Jesus Christ a
second time.

The Christians of the first centuries, feeling the importance and profit to the soul of the Holy Mysteries, used to partake of the holy Body and Blood of Christ every Sunday and every festival; and that is why among them there was, as we are told in the Book of Acts, one heart and one soul (Acts 4:32). But what a difference there is between them and us! How many nowadays have not taken communion for several years! How many people there are who have no intention of doing so!

And so, for God's sake, have a desire to communicate of the Holy Mysteries, at least once a year; every one of us should do this without fail. For those who are worthy, the Body and Blood of Christ is a true cure for all infirmities and sicknesses. And who of us is perfectly healthy? And who does not wish to obtain relief and healing? The Body and Blood of our Lord Jesus Christ is food for the journey to the heavenly kingdom. Is it possible to go on a long and difficult journey without food? The Body and Blood of Jesus Christ is the visible holy of holies, bequeathed and left to us by Jesus Christ Himself for our sanctification. Who would not wish to be a partaker of such holiness and be sanctified? And so, do not be too lazy to approach the cup of life, immortality, love, and holiness. But approach with the fear of God and with faith. And whoever does not wish to approach, but neglects to do so, does not love Jesus Christ and will not receive the Holy Spirit, and, consequently, he will not enter the kingdom of heaven.

These, then, are the ways of receiving the Holy Spirit: that is, purity of heart and integrity of life, humility, attentive listening to the voice of God, prayer, self-denial, reading and listening to the Word of God, and communion of the Body and Blood of Christ. Of course, each of these means is effectual for receiving the Holy Spirit, but the best and surest way is to use them all together; then you will undoubtedly receive the Holy Spirit and become holy.

Here it needs to be said further that if any one of you receives the Holy Spirit and then somehow falls and sins, and thereby loses the Holy Spirit, do not despair and think that all is lost; but quickly and fervently fall down before God with penitence and prayer, and the Holy Spirit will return to you again.

## POINTS OF REFLECTION

1. St Innocent describes in considerable detail how essential it is to have the Holy Spirit within us. What are the seven indications he gives of the presence of the Holy Spirit within the believer?

2. In order to receive the Holy Spirit, what should we do?

3. What are the different ways that St Innocent lists for us to receive the Holy Spirit?

4. What should we never do if, because of our sin, we drive the Holy Spirit away from us?

# CONCLUSION

Now, as far as I could, I have shown you the way into the heavenly kingdom, and you can now see for yourselves that the following are true:

1. Without faith in Jesus Christ, no one can return to God and enter the kingdom of heaven.
2. No one, even though he believes in Jesus Christ, can be called a disciple of Jesus Christ or live with Him in heaven, unless he acts and lives as Jesus Christ acted and lived on earth.
3. No one can follow Jesus Christ without the help of the Holy Spirit.
4. Whoever wishes to receive the Holy Spirit must use the means given us by the Lord for that purpose.

And I shall again repeat that the way into the heavenly kingdom revealed to us by Jesus Christ is unique and that there is not and was not and never will be another way besides the one that Jesus Christ has shown us. The way is difficult, but, it leads straight to true and eternal happiness. Although the way to the kingdom of heaven is difficult, yet not only along the way but even at the very beginning of it one meets with such consolations and delights as are never found on the path of worldly life. Trying and difficult is the way into the heavenly kingdom, but the Lord's help is ever at hand. Our Lord Jesus Christ is always ready to help us to follow Him. He gives us the Holy Spirit, and sends His angels to guard us on the way, and supplies us with teachers and guides. And He is even ready Himself to take us by the hand, so to speak, and to support us. The way into the kingdom of heaven is difficult and there are bitter labors on it, but he who has not seen and experienced what is bitter cannot know the value of what is sweet. The way into the kingdom of heaven is difficult, but while suffering here on earth we can always pray and in prayer find comfort and strength, and God always hears our prayer. But when we die not as Christians, even if we could pray there, God would not hear us. The way into the kingdom of heaven is difficult, but the eternal sufferings and torments are incomparably greater and more grievous than earthly sufferings. Even our most grievous sufferings here below, in comparison with the sufferings of hell prepared for the devil and his angels, are so small that they are like tiny drops in comparison with the whole ocean. The way to heavenly beatitude is difficult, but are the ways to earthly fortune or happiness easier? Look how those labor and sweat who make money and seek earthly honor and glory, and how often we willingly and gladly undertake labors and cares for some empty pleasure. But what is the result? Instead of receiving pleasure we only lose time, waste money, ruin our health, and destroy our soul. Therefore, if we examine ourselves more attentively, it becomes clear that it is not because the way is difficult that we do not go into the heavenly kingdom but because we have no real desire or inclination to do so, and do not want to trouble ourselves about it. Whoever ardently desires anything will always seek it, in spite of all difficulties and obstacles. Of course, there is no one who would not desire to be in the heavenly kingdom, but this desire is feeble and is only a certain inborn desire for happiness. And indeed, some of us do labor for the heavenly kingdom. But how few labor with full faith and surrender to God and true self-denial! But how many of us there are who think that however you live in this world, you only have to repent at the end of your life and you will be in the kingdom of Heaven! Oh, how terribly mistaken are those who think thus! Certainly the mercy of God is great and infinite. Jesus Christ took into paradise even a robber, who repented only when he was actually dying. But was it without suffering and without affliction that the robber entered paradise? No! He was hung on a cross. Before that he had been judged; he was locked up in prison, and perhaps he was scourged, too. True, he suffered as an evildoer and criminal. But who of us has not broken both the divine law and human laws? If we do not kill people such as robbers, yet how many people do we kill by our word, by our cruelty, and by our negligence concerning their well-being and salvation? Certainly the Lord can show us the same great and unspeakable mercies; He can regard our last sufferings as a purification and as a kind of struggle on the way to the heavenly kingdom, especially when, as with the robber, we at the same time offer repentance for our sins and receive with faith the last sacraments. But who can be sure that when we die we shall suffer and that in our suffering we shall have time to repent? How many people die suddenly and without any suffering? How many die without repentance and the last sacraments?

And so, brethren, if you do not desire eternal perdition for yourself, you must attend to your soul and take thought for your future lot. We know that there beyond the grave one or the other future awaits all alike and that there is no intermediate state, that is, that either the kingdom of heaven or hell awaits us, eternal beatitude or eternal torment. There are only two different states beyond the grave, and also only two ways here on earth. One way is broad, smooth, level, and easy, and many follow it; the other way is narrow, thorny, and difficult. Happy, a thousand times happy, is he who treads the narrow way, for it leads to the kingdom of heaven. But how few there are who go by this way! If we do not go by the difficult way, and if we die without any purification and repentance, what will happen to us? To whom shall we have recourse? To the Lord? But we do not wish to listen to Him here, and He will not listen to us there. Now He is a most merciful Father to us, but there He is the just Judge. And who will defend us from His just anger? O brethren, "it is a fearful thing to fall into the hands of the living God" (Heb 10:31)! And so, look to your salvation, while you still have an acceptable time; work and labor for your salvation while it is yet day, for the night will come, and then no one can work. Do not put it off from day to day, but hasten to the heavenly kingdom while it is still possible; for death will come, and then it will be too late. Get going somehow or other to the kingdom of heaven, and then you will gradually be getting nearer to it, even though it is slow work—just as when a person who is going somewhere takes a step forward, he gets nearer his destination.

Whoever wishes to follow Jesus Christ can make use of the following counsels:

1. Do not take any notice of how other sinful people live, and do not justify yourself by their example, and do not speak as many do: "What am I to do? I am not the only person who lives like this, and I am not the only one who does not carry out Christ's commandments, but practically everyone does the same." But even if you truly knew that all who live around

you, and even those who ought to be an example of virtue and piety, do not live in a Christian manner, what good would it be to you? Their perdition will not save you. It will be no defense for you at the awful judgment that not only you lived badly on earth. And therefore it is not your business whether they are on the way to the kingdom or not; it is not your business. Attend to yourself and to those whom God has given you to instruct. We see people sinning often enough, but we hardly ever see them repenting and purifying themselves of their sins; that is why we can so often be mistaken as to who of our neighbors is following Christ or not.

2. When you go by this way, many people, and perhaps even your nearest and dearest, will laugh at you. Do not pay any attention to that and do not worry. Remember that they also laughed at Jesus Christ. But He did not show enmity toward them; He was silent and prayed for them. You should act in exactly the same way.

3. There are many educated people who do not view aright the way into the heavenly kingdom shown us by Jesus Christ, the Son of God, and say that even without this way it is possible to attain to the heavenly kingdom, and this way is not for all, but for a few. But if you happen to meet a person of this sort and he stops you and gives you advice, do not listen to him; and even if an angel were to descend from

heaven and tell you that it is not necessary to go the way Jesus Christ went, do not listen to him either. But do not quarrel with deceivers and enemies of this kind; rather, pity and pray for them.

4. When you are firmly following Jesus Christ, perhaps you will meet people who will revile you on account of the Word of the Lord or will slander, insult, and despise you. Be patient and endure it. Rejoice and leap for joy on the day you receive any offense or wrong for the name of Christ, for great is your reward in heaven.

5. When you are truly going this way, the devil himself will rise up against you and tempt you with various temptations; he will suggest bad thoughts to you, or doubt concerning the faith itself and revealed truths, or even blasphemy. Do not be afraid of him, because the devil can do nothing to you without God's permission, and you have only to pray to the Lord and the devil will fly from you like an arrow.

6. You should take note that what is regarded as useful and just, and is actually so, does not hinder the true Christian. Such is, first of all, hard work, which not only does not hinder the salvation of the soul but even assists it. It is well known that idleness is the mother of vices. What, for instance, causes people to become drunkards? Idleness. Who are thieves and robbers? Idle people; and so forth. And it can be said for certain that a person who does nothing and has nothing

with which to occupy himself, even though he seems good, is a bad Christian and a bad citizen; and if he is not a great sinner, that is only because of God's special care of him. And so, be industrious, accustom yourself to work, toil and labor, and do all that is useful and necessary for your home, and all that is your duty to your king and country. If idleness is the mother of vice, industry may be called the father of virtue. This is so, first, because an industrious person is certain to have fewer sins, simply because he has no time not only to do evil but to think of evil; for he is either working and busy doing his duty or he is occupied with his salvation and his duties as a Christian. Second, it is true because a person who is in the habit of being industrious will sooner agree to go the way to the kingdom of heaven than a person who leads an idle life, and it is easier for an industrious person to go the way to the kingdom of heaven than for an idle person. To be industrious is always and everywhere profitable. But to be industrious, you must train yourself and accustom yourself to work from childhood.

7. There is another perfection just as valuable as diligence to which you should train and accustom yourself even before diligence. This is patience or endurance. Patience is always and everywhere useful, but for a person who wishes to go into the kingdom of heaven, patience is a most indispensable perfection. Without patience, you cannot even take a step

on this way, because at every step you are bound to meet roughness and unevenness and thorniness.

8. And so, train and accustom yourself to patience, first bodily and then spiritual. Then it will be easier for you to be both an industrious member of society and a good friend, and a good housekeeper, and a good citizen, and a good Christian.

Now I have told you all I can concerning the way into the heavenly kingdom. I shall only add that a person who goes the way into the heavenly kingdom fervently, for every labor, for every sorrow, for every victory over himself and for every restraint of himself, for every act and even for every good desire and intention, will be rewarded seventy times sevenfold even in this life, and what awaits him there cannot be told or imagined. And so, do not be afraid to follow Jesus Christ; He is a powerful Helper; follow Him, hasten and do not delay. Go while the doors into the heavenly kingdom are still open to you. And even while you are still a long way off, our heavenly Father will come to meet you on the way, will kiss you, will put on you the best garment, and will lead you into His bridal-chamber where He Himself dwells with all the holy prophets, apostles, martyrs, and all the saints, and where you will rejoice with true and eternal joy. But when the doors of the heavenly kingdom are closed to you, that is, if you die without repentance and good works, then however much you may want and however much you may try to enter, you will not be admitted. You will knock at the doors and say, "Lord, open to us! We know Thee, we were baptized in Thy name, we are called by Thy name and have even worked miracles by it." But Jesus Christ will say to you, "I do not know you, you are not Mine! Depart from Me into the eternal fire prepared for the devil and his angels." Then there will be weeping and gnashing of teeth.

## POINTS OF REFLECTION

1. How does St Innocent summarize the way to the heavenly kingdom?

2. Is it easier to seek happiness here and now rather than striving for the kingdom of heaven?

3. Is it wise to put off living for God to later in life in the belief that we can repent shortly before our death and be saved?

4. If we see that others sin, including those who we expect to set an example for us, does this give us reason not to do good ourselves?

5. What is "the mother of vice" and what is "the father of virtue"?

Saint Innocent
Metropolitan of Moscow and Apostle to America